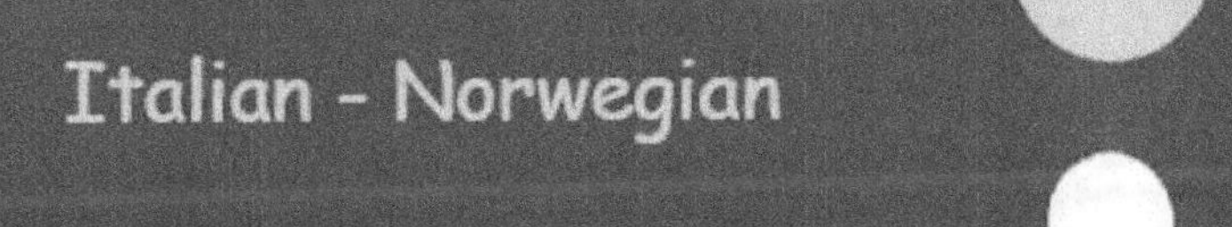

Italian - Norwegian

Teach Your Child to Read

700 Short Easy Sentences

Name

I Can...

- [ ] read the 1st sentence.
- [ ] read the 2nd sentence.
- [ ] read the 3rd sentence.
- [ ] make my own sentence.
- [ ] color a picture.

La rana sta andando a una festa.

Frosken skal på fest.

The frog is going to a party.

La rana verde indossa un cappello verde.

Den grønne frosken har på seg en grønn hatt.

The green frog is wearing a green hat.

Name

I Can...

- [ ] read the 1st sentence.
- [ ] read the 2nd sentence.
- [ ] read the 3rd sentence.
- [ ] make my own sentence.
- [ ] color a picture.

A Gufo piace leggere grandi libri.

Uglen liker å lese store bøker.

Owl likes to read big books.

Il giovane gufo marrone sta imparando a leggere.

Den unge brune uglen lærer å lese.

The young brown owl is learning to read.

Name

I Can...

- [ ] read the 1st sentence.
- [ ] read the 2nd sentence.
- [ ] read the 3rd sentence.
- [ ] make my own sentence.
- [ ] color a picture.

Dai! Il camion dei gelati è qui!

Kom igjen! Isbilen er her!

Come on! The ice cream truck is here!

Il camion dei gelati sta suonando una bellissima canzone.

Isbilen spiller en vakker sang.

The ice cream truck is playing a beautiful song.

Name

I Can...

- [ ] read the 1st sentence.
- [ ] read the 2nd sentence.
- [ ] read the 3rd sentence.
- [ ] make my own sentence.
- [ ] color a picture.

I draghi sono molto amichevoli e hanno delle scale sulla schiena.

Drager er veldig vennlige og har vekter på ryggen.

Dragons are very friendly and have scales on their backs.

Il grande drago antico ti saluta.

Den store gamle dragen sier hei til deg.

The big ancient dragon says hello to you.

Name

I Can...

- [ ] read the 1st sentence.
- [ ] read the 2nd sentence.
- [ ] read the 3rd sentence.
- [ ] make my own sentence.
- [ ] color a picture.

Questo ariete vive nella fattoria.

Denne rammen bor i våningshuset.

This ram lives in the farmhouse.

Il montone sorride perché ha appena fatto il bagno.

Rammen smiler fordi den bare tok et bad.

The ram is smiling because it just took a bath.

Name ________________

I Can...

- ☐ read the 1st sentence.
- ☐ read the 2nd sentence.
- ☐ read the 3rd sentence.
- ☐ make my own sentence.
- ☐ color a picture.

Al coniglietto piace mangiare le carote.

Bunny liker å spise gulrøtter.

The bunny likes to eat carrots.

Il coniglietto sta portando una carota gigante alla sua famiglia per cena.

Bunnyen tar med seg en gigantisk gulrot til familien til middag.

The bunny is bringing a giant carrot to its family for dinner.

Name _______________________

I Can...

- [ ] read the 1st sentence.
- [ ] read the 2nd sentence.
- [ ] read the 3rd sentence.
- [ ] make my own sentence.
- [ ] color a picture.

Al pagliaccio piace distribuire palloncini ai più piccoli.

Klovnen liker å gi ut ballonger til små barn.

The clown likes to give out balloons to little kids.

Il pagliaccio tiene in mano tre palloncini colorati.

Klovnen holder tre fargerike ballonger.

The clown is holding three colorful balloons.

Name _______________________ 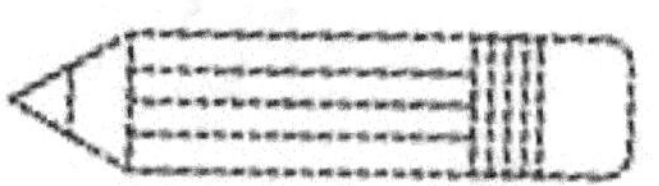

I Can...

- [ ] read the 1st sentence.
- [ ] read the 2nd sentence.
- [ ] read the 3rd sentence.
- [ ] make my own sentence.
- [ ] color a picture.

Il pagliaccio si destreggia tra le palle per la sua esibizione.

Klovnen sjonglerer baller for sin prestasjon.

The clown is juggling balls for his performance.

Il buffo clown si destreggia con abilità.

Den morsomme klovnen sjonglerer med dyktighet.

The funny clown is juggling with skill.

Name

I Can...

- [ ] read the 1st sentence.
- [ ] read the 2nd sentence.
- [ ] read the 3rd sentence.
- [ ] make my own sentence.
- [ ] color a picture.

Il coniglietto pasquale distribuirà le uova di cioccolato.

Påskeharen kommer til å gi ut sjokoladeegg.

The Easter Bunny is going to give out chocolate eggs.

Il coniglio ha appena strappato alcune carote dal giardino.

Kaninen plukket bare noen gulrøtter ut av hagen.

The rabbit just plucked some carrots out of the garden.

I Can...

- [ ] read the 1st sentence.
- [ ] read the 2nd sentence.
- [ ] read the 3rd sentence.
- [ ] make my own sentence.
- [ ] color a picture.

La matita disegna una linea a zig-zag.

Blyanten tegner en sikksakk-linje.

The pencil is drawing a zig-zag line.

La matita sta scrivendo una linea con il piombo.

Blyanten skritter en linje med ledningen.

The pencil is scribbling a line with the lead.

Name 

I Can...

- [ ] read the 1st sentence.
- [ ] read the 2nd sentence.
- [ ] read the 3rd sentence.
- [ ] make my own sentence.
- [ ] color a picture.

La matita fece un grande sorriso e andò a lavorare.

Blyanten la på seg et stort smil og gikk på jobb.

The pencil put on a big smile and went to work.

La matita si sveglia brillante e presto per andare al lavoro.

Blyanten våkner lyst og tidlig for å gå på jobb.

The pencil wakes up bright and early to go to work.

Name

I Can...

- [ ] read the 1st sentence.
- [ ] read the 2nd sentence.
- [ ] read the 3rd sentence.
- [ ] make my own sentence.
- [ ] color a picture.

Questo pupazzo di neve è mio amico ed è un aiutante di Babbo Natale.

Denne snømannen er min venn, og han er en hjelper til julenissen.

This snowman is my friend, and he is a helper of Santa.

Il pupazzo di neve sta organizzando una festa di Natale.

Snømannen holder julebord.

The snowman is having a Christmas party.

Name _______________________ 

I Can...

- [ ] read the 1st sentence.
- [ ] read the 2nd sentence.
- [ ] read the 3rd sentence.
- [ ] make my own sentence.
- [ ] color a picture.

Il polpo lavora come chef e serve cibo.

Blekkspruten jobber som kokk og serverer mat.

The octopus is working as a chef and serving food.

Il polpo cucinava cibo delizioso per i suoi amici.

Blekkspruten tilberedte deilig mat til vennene sine.

The octopus cooked delicious food for its friends.

Name ______________________ 

I Can...

- [ ] read the 1st sentence.
- [ ] read the 2nd sentence.
- [ ] read the 3rd sentence.
- [ ] make my own sentence.
- [ ] color a picture.

Babbo Natale è felice.

Julenissen er fornøyd.

Santa is happy.

Babbo Natale consegna regali ai bambini.

Julenissen leverer gaver til barna.

Santa Claus is delivering presents to the children.

Name

I Can...

- [ ] read the 1st sentence.
- [ ] read the 2nd sentence.
- [ ] read the 3rd sentence.
- [ ] make my own sentence.
- [ ] color a picture.

All'orso piace mangiare dolci.

Bjørnen spiser søtsaker.

The bear likes to eat sweets.

L'orsacchiotto marrone indossa un cappello verde brillante.

Den brune bamsen har en lysegrønn hatt på.

The brown teddy bear is wearing a bright green hat.

Name ____________________ 

I Can...

- [ ] read the 1st sentence.
- [ ] read the 2nd sentence.
- [ ] read the 3rd sentence.
- [ ] make my own sentence.
- [ ] color a picture.

Il libro ha una bacchetta.

Boken har et tryllestav.

The book has a wand.

Il ragazzo ha ricevuto un personaggio da mago per il suo compleanno.

Gutten fikk en trollmannshandling for bursdagen sin.

The boy got a wizard action figure for his birthday.

Name 

I Can...

- [ ] read the 1st sentence.
- [ ] read the 2nd sentence.
- [ ] read the 3rd sentence.
- [ ] make my own sentence.
- [ ] color a picture.

L'orso ha un regalo.

Bjørnen har en gave.

The bear has a present.

L'orsacchiotto sta aprendo il suo secondo regalo.

Bamsen åpner sin andre gave.

The teddy bear is opening his second present.

Name ____________________

I Can...

- [ ] read the 1st sentence.
- [ ] read the 2nd sentence.
- [ ] read the 3rd sentence.
- [ ] make my own sentence.
- [ ] color a picture.

Babbo Natale distribuirà regali.

Julenissen kommer til å gi gaver.

Santa is going to give out presents.

Babbo Natale porta una borsa di pelle piena di regali.

Julenissen har med seg en skinnveske fylt med gaver.

Santa Claus is carrying a leather bag filled with gifts.

Name

I Can...

- [ ] read the 1st sentence.
- [ ] read the 2nd sentence.
- [ ] read the 3rd sentence.
- [ ] make my own sentence.
- [ ] color a picture.

Ho fatto un pupazzo di neve.

Jeg laget en snømann.

I made a snowman.

Il pupazzo di neve aveva appena finito di pulire il cortile.

Snømannen var akkurat ferdig med å rense hagen.

The snowman was just done cleaning the yard.

I Can...

- [ ] read the 1st sentence.
- [ ] read the 2nd sentence.
- [ ] read the 3rd sentence.
- [ ] make my own sentence.
- [ ] color a picture.

Il pappagallo è colorato.

Papegøyen er fargerik.

The parrot is colorful.

Il pappagallo sta solo imparando a volare nel cielo.

Papegøyen lærer bare à fly på himmelen.

The parrot is just learning how to fly in the sky.

Name _______________________

I Can...

- [ ] read the 1st sentence.
- [ ] read the 2nd sentence.
- [ ] read the 3rd sentence.
- [ ] make my own sentence.
- [ ] color a picture.

Ci sono molti animali

Det er mange dyr.

There are a lot of animals.

Gli animali stanno avendo un pigiama party gigante.

Dyrene får en enorm søvn.

The animals are having a giant sleepover.

Name

I Can...

- [ ] read the 1st sentence.
- [ ] read the 2nd sentence.
- [ ] read the 3rd sentence.
- [ ] make my own sentence.
- [ ] color a picture.

L'uomo indossa una cintura.

Mannen har belte på seg.

The man is wearing a belt.

L'uomo verrà a riparare la nave.

Mannen kommer for å fikse skipet.

The man is coming to fix the ship.

Name

I Can...

- [ ] read the 1st sentence.
- [ ] read the 2nd sentence.
- [ ] read the 3rd sentence.
- [ ] make my own sentence.
- [ ] color a picture.

Il coniglio è molto giovane

Kaninen er veldig ung.

The rabbit is very young.

Il mago evocò un coniglio dal suo cappello.

Trollmannen tilkalte en kanin ut av hatten.

The magician summoned a rabbit out of his hat.

Name

I Can...

- [ ] read the 1st sentence.
- [ ] read the 2nd sentence.
- [ ] read the 3rd sentence.
- [ ] make my own sentence.
- [ ] color a picture.

Ha una pozione.

Han har en potion.

He has a potion.

La donna sta imparando a diventare una scienziata.

Kvinnen lærer å bli forsker.

The woman is learning how to become a scientist.

Name ___________________ 

I Can...

- [ ] read the 1st sentence.
- [ ] read the 2nd sentence.
- [ ] read the 3rd sentence.
- [ ] make my own sentence.
- [ ] color a picture.

Indossa occhiali da sole.

Han har på seg solbriller.

He is wearing sunglasses.

Il poliziotto è arrabbiato con alcuni adolescenti marci.

Politimannen er sint på noen råtne tenåringer.

The policeman is angry at some rotten teenagers.

Name _______________________ 

I Can...

- [ ] read the 1st sentence.
- [ ] read the 2nd sentence.
- [ ] read the 3rd sentence.
- [ ] make my own sentence.
- [ ] color a picture.

Ha un secchio di vernice.

Han har en bøtte med maling.

He has a bucket of paint.

Il pittore di casa ha quasi finito con il suo lavoro quotidiano.

Husmaleren er nesten ferdig med sitt daglige arbeid.

The house painter is almost done with his daily work.

Name

I Can...

- [ ] read the 1st sentence.
- [ ] read the 2nd sentence.
- [ ] read the 3rd sentence.
- [ ] make my own sentence.
- [ ] color a picture.

L'uomo ha un cappello.

Mannen har hatt.

The man has a hat.

Il postino consegna le poste all'alba.

Postmannen leverer post i daggryssprikken.

The postman is delivering mails at the crack of dawn.

Name

I Can...

- [ ] read the 1st sentence.
- [ ] read the 2nd sentence.
- [ ] read the 3rd sentence.
- [ ] make my own sentence.
- [ ] color a picture.

Ha un walkie-talkie.

Han har en walkie talkie.

He has a walkie talkie.

L'uomo d'affari chiama il suo capo.

Forretningsmannen ringer sjefen sin.

The businessman is calling his boss.

Name _______________________

I Can...

- [ ] read the 1st sentence.
- [ ] read the 2nd sentence.
- [ ] read the 3rd sentence.
- [ ] make my own sentence.
- [ ] color a picture.

Ha sonno.

Han er søvnig.

He is sleepy.

L'operaio sta rimorchiando delle scatole pesanti.

Arbeidsmannen sleper noen tunge kasser.

The workman is towing some heavy boxes.

Name _______________________

I Can...

- [ ] read the 1st sentence.
- [ ] read the 2nd sentence.
- [ ] read the 3rd sentence.
- [ ] make my own sentence.
- [ ] color a picture.

Indossa una cravatta a farfalla.

Han har på seg bowie.

He is wearing a bowtie.

Il cameriere serve limonata fresca a una famiglia.

The waiter serverer fersk limonade til en familie.

The waiter is serving fresh lemonade to a family.

Name ___________

I Can...

- [ ] read the 1st sentence.
- [ ] read the 2nd sentence.
- [ ] read the 3rd sentence.
- [ ] make my own sentence.
- [ ] color a picture.

Lui ha una valigia.

Han har koffert.

He has a suitcase.

L'ingegnere riparerà un'auto blu di fantasia.

Ingeniøren skal fikse en fancy blå bil.

The engineer is going to fix a fancy blue car.

Name

I Can...

- [ ] read the 1st sentence.
- [ ] read the 2nd sentence.
- [ ] read the 3rd sentence.
- [ ] make my own sentence.
- [ ] color a picture.

Lo chef ha un tovagliolo.

Kokken har et serviett.

The chef has a napkin.

Lo chef ha preparato una deliziosa pasta che tutti possono condividere.

Kokken lagde kjempegod pasta for alle å dele.

The chef made yummy pasta for everyone to share.

Name ___________________ 

I Can...

- [ ] read the 1st sentence.
- [ ] read the 2nd sentence.
- [ ] read the 3rd sentence.
- [ ] make my own sentence.
- [ ] color a picture.

Il gallo ha un grosso becco.

Hanen har et stort nebb.

The rooster has a big beak.

Il pollo bianco indossa un cappello da artista.

Den hvite kyllingen har på seg en kunstnerhatt.

The white chicken is wearing an artist's hat.

Name

I Can...

- [ ] read the 1st sentence.
- [ ] read the 2nd sentence.
- [ ] read the 3rd sentence.
- [ ] make my own sentence.
- [ ] color a picture.

L'uccello è piccolo.

Fuglen er liten.

The bird is small.

Il piccolo pulcino sta usando il telefono di sua madre per riprodurre musica.

Den lille kyllingen bruker sin mors telefon for å spille musikk.

The little chick is using his mother's phone to play music.

I Can...

- [ ] read the 1st sentence.
- [ ] read the 2nd sentence.
- [ ] read the 3rd sentence.
- [ ] make my own sentence.
- [ ] color a picture.

Questo è il mio anello.

Det er ringen min.

That is my ring.

L'anello ha un gioiello di diamanti.

Ringen har en diamantjuvel på seg.

The ring has a diamond jewel on it.

Name

I Can...

- [ ] read the 1st sentence.
- [ ] read the 2nd sentence.
- [ ] read the 3rd sentence.
- [ ] make my own sentence.
- [ ] color a picture.

L'anatra ha tre uova.

Anda har tre egg.

The duck has three eggs.

L'anatra ha appena lasciato cadere le sue piccole uova ovali.

Anda droppet bare de små ovale eggene sine.

The duck just dropped its little oval eggs.

Name 

I Can...

- [ ] read the 1st sentence.
- [ ] read the 2nd sentence.
- [ ] read the 3rd sentence.
- [ ] make my own sentence.
- [ ] color a picture.

Il cigno è bellissimo.

Svanen er vakker.

The swan is beautiful.

Il bellissimo cigno sta mangiando un pezzo di verdure verdi.

Den vakre svanen spiser et stykke grønne grønnsaker.

The beautiful swan is eating a piece of green vegetables.

Name _______________

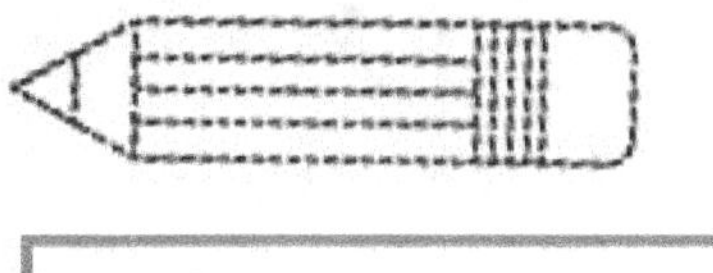

I Can...

- [ ] read the 1st sentence.
- [ ] read the 2nd sentence.
- [ ] read the 3rd sentence.
- [ ] make my own sentence.
- [ ] color a picture.

La ragazza indossa un vestito.

Jenta har på seg en kjole.

The girl is wearing a dress.

La bambina porta due secchi carichi d'acqua.

Den lille jenta har to vann med bøtter.

The little girl is carrying two buckets loads of water.

Name

I Can...

- [ ] read the 1st sentence.
- [ ] read the 2nd sentence.
- [ ] read the 3rd sentence.
- [ ] make my own sentence.
- [ ] color a picture.

Il ragazzo sta correndo.

Gutten løper.

The boy is running.

Il velocista sta conquistando il primo posto in una gara.

Sprinteren vinner førsteplassen i et løp.

The sprinter is winning first place in a race.

Name

I Can...

- [ ] read the 1st sentence.
- [ ] read the 2nd sentence.
- [ ] read the 3rd sentence.
- [ ] make my own sentence.
- [ ] color a picture.

Lui è un musicista.

Han er musiker.

He is a musician.

Il ragazzo sta esercitando il flauto per essere pronto a scuola.

Gutten øver på fløyten for å være klar på skolen.

The boy is practicing the flute to be ready at school.

Name ____________________

I Can...

- [ ] read the 1st sentence.
- [ ] read the 2nd sentence.
- [ ] read the 3rd sentence.
- [ ] make my own sentence.
- [ ] color a picture.

Sembra gioioso.

Han ser glad ut.

He looks joyful.

Il batterista sta conducendo una grande parata in costume.

I rommeslageren leder en enorm draktparade.

The drummer is leading a huge costume parade.

Name _______________________

I Can...

- [ ] read the 1st sentence.
- [ ] read the 2nd sentence.
- [ ] read the 3rd sentence.
- [ ] make my own sentence.
- [ ] color a picture.

Il dinosauro è una rock star.

Dinosauren er en rockestjerne.

The dinosaur is a rock star.

Il sogno del dinosauro è quello di diventare una rockstar meravigliosa.

Dinosaurens drøm er å bli en fantastisk rockestjerne.

The dinosaur's dream is to become a wonderful rock star.

Name

I Can...

- [ ] read the 1st sentence.
- [ ] read the 2nd sentence.
- [ ] read the 3rd sentence.
- [ ] make my own sentence.
- [ ] color a picture.

L'infermiera aiuta il medico.

Sykepleieren hjelper legen.

The nurse helps the doctor.

L'infermiera aiuta i pazienti a stare meglio.

Sykepleieren hjelper pasienter med å bli bedre.

The nurse is helping patients get better.

Name

I Can...

- [ ] read the 1st sentence.
- [ ] read the 2nd sentence.
- [ ] read the 3rd sentence.
- [ ] make my own sentence.
- [ ] color a picture.

Indossa una corona.

Hun har på seg en krone.

She is wearing a crown.

L'alveare ha un leader che è un'ape magica.

Bikupen har en leder som er en magisk bie.

The beehive has a leader who is a magical bee.

Name

I Can...

- [ ] read the 1st sentence.
- [ ] read the 2nd sentence.
- [ ] read the 3rd sentence.
- [ ] make my own sentence.
- [ ] color a picture.

È arancione e nero.

Den er oransje og svart.

It is orange and black.

Una tigre formale sta agitando la mano per un taxi giallo.

En formell tiger vifter med hånden etter en gul taxi.

A formal tiger is waving his hand for a yellow taxi.

Name 

I Can...

- [ ] read the 1st sentence.
- [ ] read the 2nd sentence.
- [ ] read the 3rd sentence.
- [ ] make my own sentence.
- [ ] color a picture.

Il ragazzo porta molti libri.

Gutten har mange bøker på seg.

The boy is carrying a lot of books.

Il ragazzino intelligente porta libri pesanti da studiare.

Den smarte lille gutten bærer tunge bøker for å studere.

The smart little boy is carrying heavy books to study.

Name

I Can...

- [ ] read the 1st sentence.
- [ ] read the 2nd sentence.
- [ ] read the 3rd sentence.
- [ ] make my own sentence.
- [ ] color a picture.

La pizza sembra deliziosa.

Pizzaen ser deilig ut.

The pizza looks delicious.

Lo chef ha appena preso il forno per la pizza

Kokken tok nettopp pizzaovnen

The chef just took the pizza oven

Name

I Can...

- [ ] read the 1st sentence.
- [ ] read the 2nd sentence.
- [ ] read the 3rd sentence.
- [ ] make my own sentence.
- [ ] color a picture.

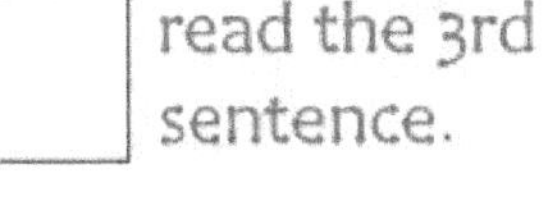

Questo è il computer di mio padre.

Det er datamaskinen til faren min.

That is my dad's computer.

Il laptop sta salutando l'utente.

Den bærbare datamaskinen sier hei til brukeren.

The laptop is saying hi to the user.

Name

I Can...

- [ ] read the 1st sentence.
- [ ] read the 2nd sentence.
- [ ] read the 3rd sentence.
- [ ] make my own sentence.
- [ ] color a picture.

Il contadino ha la barba.

Bonden har skjegg.

The farmer has a beard.

Il giardiniere pianterà dei semi.

Gartneren skal plante noen frø.

The gardener is going to plant some seeds.

Name

I Can...

- [ ] read the 1st sentence.
- [ ] read the 2nd sentence.
- [ ] read the 3rd sentence.
- [ ] make my own sentence.
- [ ] color a picture.

La fragola è rossa

Jordbæren er rød.

The strawberry is red.

La fragola beve succo freddo rinfrescante.

Jordbæren drikker kald forfriskende juice.

The strawberry is drinking cold refreshing juice.

Name

I Can...

- [ ] read the 1st sentence.
- [ ] read the 2nd sentence.
- [ ] read the 3rd sentence.
- [ ] make my own sentence.
- [ ] color a picture.

Il mago ha una bacchetta.

I rollmannen har en tryllestav.

The magician has a wand.

Il mago evocherà un grande drago.

Veiviseren skal tilkalle en flott stor drage.

The wizard is going to summon a great big dragon.

Name

I Can...

- [ ] read the 1st sentence.
- [ ] read the 2nd sentence.
- [ ] read the 3rd sentence.
- [ ] make my own sentence.
- [ ] color a picture.

La renna ha una sciarpa.

Reinsdyr har et skjerf.

Reindeer has a scarf.

La renna è in ritardo per dare il suo regalo ai suoi amici.

Reinen er sent ute med å gi sin gave til vennene sine.

The reindeer is late to give his present to his friends.

Name

I Can...

- [ ] read the 1st sentence.
- [ ] read the 2nd sentence.
- [ ] read the 3rd sentence.
- [ ] make my own sentence.
- [ ] color a picture.

Ho molte matite.

Jeg har mange blyanter.

I have a lot of pencils.

Gli utensili per la scrittura sono nel barattolo di latta.

Skriveutstyrene er i blikkboksen.

The writing utensils are in the tin can.

Name 

I Can...

- [ ] read the 1st sentence.
- [ ] read the 2nd sentence.
- [ ] read the 3rd sentence.
- [ ] make my own sentence.
- [ ] color a picture.

Babbo Natale è grasso.

Julenissen er feit.

Santa is fat.

Babbo Natale sta ridendo di una battuta esilarante.

Julenissen ler av en morsom vits.

Santa Claus is laughing at a hilarious joke.

Name

I Can...

- [ ] read the 1st sentence.
- [ ] read the 2nd sentence.
- [ ] read the 3rd sentence.
- [ ] make my own sentence.
- [ ] color a picture.

Ho un naso.

Jeg har en nese.

I have one nose.

Il numero uno ha ottenuto il primo posto in una competizione.

Nummer én fikk førsteplass på en konkurranse.

Number one got first place at a competition.

Name

I Can...

- [ ] read the 1st sentence.
- [ ] read the 2nd sentence.
- [ ] read the 3rd sentence.
- [ ] make my own sentence.
- [ ] color a picture.

Ho due orecchie.

Jeg har to ører.

I have two ears.

Il numero due è in posa per un selfie.

Nummer to poserer for en selfie.

Number two is posing for a selfie.

Name

I Can...

- [ ] read the 1st sentence.
- [ ] read the 2nd sentence.
- [ ] read the 3rd sentence.
- [ ] make my own sentence.
- [ ] color a picture.

Ho tre bottoni sul mio vestito.

Jeg har tre knapper på kjolen.

I have three buttons on my dress.

Il numero tre conta fino a tre.

Nummer tre teller til tre.

Number three is counting to three.

Name _______________________

I Can...

- [ ] read the 1st sentence.
- [ ] read the 2nd sentence.
- [ ] read the 3rd sentence.
- [ ] make my own sentence.
- [ ] color a picture.

Ho 0 code.

Jeg har 0 haler.

I have 0 tails.

Lo zero dice bene facendo il gesto giusto.

Nullen sier fint ved å gjøre den ok gesten.

The zero is saying fine by making the okay gesture.

Name

I Can...

- [ ] read the 1st sentence.
- [ ] read the 2nd sentence.
- [ ] read the 3rd sentence.
- [ ] make my own sentence.
- [ ] color a picture.

Ho cinque dita su 1 delle mie mani.

Jeg har fem fingre på 1 av hendene.

I have five fingers on 1 of my hands.

I cinque stanno dicendo il suo nome ad alta voce, quindi altri lo sapranno.

De fem sier navnet sitt høyt, så andre vil vite det.

The five are saying its name out loud, so others will know.

Name _______________________________ 

I Can...

- ☐ read the 1st sentence.
- ☐ read the 2nd sentence.
- ☐ read the 3rd sentence.
- ☐ make my own sentence.
- ☐ color a picture.

Il mio gatto ha quattro zampe.

Katten min har fire bein.

My cat has four legs.

I quattro videro quattro delfini nell'oceano.

De fire så fire delfiner ved havet.

The four saw four dolphins at the ocean.

Name

I Can...

- [ ] read the 1st sentence.
- [ ] read the 2nd sentence.
- [ ] read the 3rd sentence.
- [ ] make my own sentence.
- [ ] color a picture.

Una farfalla ha sei zampe.

En sommerfugl har seks ben.

A butterfly has six legs.

I sei saltano eccitati su e giù.

De seks hopper spent opp og ned.

The six are excitedly jumping up and down.

Name

I Can...

- [ ] read the 1st sentence.
- [ ] read the 2nd sentence.
- [ ] read the 3rd sentence.
- [ ] make my own sentence.
- [ ] color a picture.

Un ragno ha otto zampe.

En edderkopp har åtte ben.

A spider has eight legs.

L'otto si lecca il labbro perché vede otto vassoi di pollo fritto.

De åtte slikker leppen fordi den ser åtte brett med stekt kylling.

The eight is licking its lip because it sees eight trays of fried chicken.

Name

I Can...

- [ ] read the 1st sentence.
- [ ] read the 2nd sentence.
- [ ] read the 3rd sentence.
- [ ] make my own sentence.
- [ ] color a picture.

Il gallo sta per svegliare le persone.

Hanen skal vekke folk.

The rooster is going to wake people up.

Il gallo sta svegliando tutti.

Hanen våkner opp alle sammen.

The rooster is waking up everybody.

Name ____________________ 

I Can...

- [ ] read the 1st sentence.
- [ ] read the 2nd sentence.
- [ ] read the 3rd sentence.
- [ ] make my own sentence.
- [ ] color a picture.

Mia sorella ha nove animali di peluche.

Søsteren min har ni utstoppede dyr.

My sister has nine stuffed animals.

Il nove sta dicendo che 4 + 5 = 9.

De ni sier at 4 + 5 = 9.

The nine is saying that 4+5=9.

Name

I Can...

- [ ] read the 1st sentence.
- [ ] read the 2nd sentence.
- [ ] read the 3rd sentence.
- [ ] make my own sentence.
- [ ] color a picture.

L'ape baby ha strisce gialle e nere.

Babybien har gule og svarte striper.

The baby bee has yellow and black stripes.

Le api hanno ali molto piccole.

Babybiene har veldig små vinger.

The baby bees have very tiny wings.

Name

I Can...

- [ ] read the 1st sentence.
- [ ] read the 2nd sentence.
- [ ] read the 3rd sentence.
- [ ] make my own sentence.
- [ ] color a picture.

La coccinella ha molti punti.

Marihøna har mange flekker.

The ladybug has many spots.

La coccinella sta mangiando un pezzo di lattuga.

Marihøna spiser et stykke salat.

The ladybug is eating a piece of lettuce.

Name

I Can...

- [ ] read the 1st sentence.
- [ ] read the 2nd sentence.
- [ ] read the 3rd sentence.
- [ ] make my own sentence.
- [ ] color a picture.

Le pecore sono magre.

Sauene er tynne.

The sheep are skinny.

Questa pecora è così soffice.

Denne sauen er så luftig.

This sheep is so fluffy.

Name

I Can...

- [ ] read the 1st sentence.
- [ ] read the 2nd sentence.
- [ ] read the 3rd sentence.
- [ ] make my own sentence.
- [ ] color a picture.

Il coniglio partecipa a una gara di pittura di uova.

Kaninen deltar i en eggmalingskonkurranse.

The rabbit is entering an egg painting contest.

Al coniglietto pasquale piace dipingere le uova.

Påskeharen liker å male egg.

The Easter Bunny likes to paint eggs.

Name 

I Can...

- [ ] read the 1st sentence.
- [ ] read the 2nd sentence.
- [ ] read the 3rd sentence.
- [ ] make my own sentence.
- [ ] color a picture.

Il gufo è un insegnante di arti linguistiche.

Uglen er en lærer i språkkunster.

The owl is a language arts teacher.

Mr. Owl insegna in terza elementare.

Mr.Owl underviser i 3. klasse.

Mr.Owl teaches the 3rd grade.

Name ___________

I Can...

- [ ] read the 1st sentence.
- [ ] read the 2nd sentence.
- [ ] read the 3rd sentence.
- [ ] make my own sentence.
- [ ] color a picture.

L'uomo ha un martello antico.

Mannen har en eldgammel hammer.

The man has an ancient hammer.

L'uomo ha comprato un nuovo martello lucido.

Mannen har kjøpt en skinnende ny hammer.

The man has bought a shiny new hammer.

Name

I Can...

- [ ] read the 1st sentence.
- [ ] read the 2nd sentence.
- [ ] read the 3rd sentence.
- [ ] make my own sentence.
- [ ] color a picture.

La capra ha un amico.

Geiten har en venn.

The goat has a friend.

La capra ha quattro zoccoli.

Geiten har fire høver.

The goat has four hooves.

Name

I Can...

- [ ] read the 1st sentence.
- [ ] read the 2nd sentence.
- [ ] read the 3rd sentence.
- [ ] make my own sentence.
- [ ] color a picture.

L'amica di mia mamma è una domestica.

Min venns venn er en hushjelp.

My mom's friend is a maid.

La cameriera ha una grande scopa marrone.

Hushjelpen har en stor brun kost.

The maid has a big brown broom.

Name

I Can...

- [ ] read the 1st sentence.
- [ ] read the 2nd sentence.
- [ ] read the 3rd sentence.
- [ ] make my own sentence.
- [ ] color a picture.

Sono andato allo zoo.

Jeg dro til dyrehagen.

I went to the zoo.

Gli animali hanno invitato la scimmia e il pappagallo a unirsi al loro pigiama party.

Dyrene inviterte apen og papegøyen til å bli med på søvn.

The animals invited the monkey and the parrot to join their sleepover.

Name _______________________ 

I Can...

- [ ] read the 1st sentence.
- [ ] read the 2nd sentence.
- [ ] read the 3rd sentence.
- [ ] make my own sentence.
- [ ] color a picture.

Il dinosauro ha un cuscino.

Dinosauren har en pute.

The dinosaur has a pillow.

Il dinosauro sta ottenendo un piatto per il suo cibo.

Dinosauren skaffer seg en tallerken for maten.

The dinosaur is getting a plate for his food.

Name ____________________ 

I Can...

- [ ] read the 1st sentence.
- [ ] read the 2nd sentence.
- [ ] read the 3rd sentence.
- [ ] make my own sentence.
- [ ] color a picture.

Il ragazzo è entusiasta di andare a scuola.

Gutten er spent på å gå på skolen.

The boy is excited to go to school.

Il ragazzo si sta preparando per la scuola.

Gutten forbereder seg på skolen.

The boy is preparing for school.

Name

I Can...

- [ ] read the 1st sentence.
- [ ] read the 2nd sentence.
- [ ] read the 3rd sentence.
- [ ] make my own sentence.
- [ ] color a picture.

I bambini sullo scuolabus vanno a scuola.

Barna på skolebussen skal på skolen.

The kids on the school bus are going to school.

I bambini vanno a scuola su un autobus.

Barna går på skole på buss.

The children go to school on a bus.

Name ____________________ 

I Can...

- [ ] read the 1st sentence.
- [ ] read the 2nd sentence.
- [ ] read the 3rd sentence.
- [ ] make my own sentence.
- [ ] color a picture.

Il cobra è adorabile.

Kobraen er veldig deilig.

The cobra is very lovely.

L'anaconda è il serpente più lungo del mondo.

Anacondaen er den lengste slangen i verden.

The anaconda is the longest snake in the world.

Name

I Can...

- [ ] read the 1st sentence.
- [ ] read the 2nd sentence.
- [ ] read the 3rd sentence.
- [ ] make my own sentence.
- [ ] color a picture.

Questo è un cane grasso!

Det er en feit hund!

That is a fat dog!

Il cane ha un colletto d'oro.

Hunden har en gylden krage.

The dog has a golden collar.

Name

I Can...

- [ ] read the 1st sentence.
- [ ] read the 2nd sentence.
- [ ] read the 3rd sentence.
- [ ] make my own sentence.
- [ ] color a picture.

L'elefante vive nello zoo.

Elefanten bor i dyrehagen.

The elephant lives in the zoo.

L'elefante ha un tronco lungo.

Elefanten har en lang bagasjerom.

The elephant has a long trunk.

Name ________________________

I Can...

- [ ] read the 1st sentence.
- [ ] read the 2nd sentence.
- [ ] read the 3rd sentence.
- [ ] make my own sentence.
- [ ] color a picture.

La giraffa mangia verdure.

Sjiraffen spiser grønnsaker.

The giraffe eats vegetables.

La giraffa ha molti punti.

Sjiraffen har mange flekker.

The giraffe has many spots.

Name _______________________

I Can...

- [ ] read the 1st sentence.
- [ ] read the 2nd sentence.
- [ ] read the 3rd sentence.
- [ ] make my own sentence.
- [ ] color a picture.

Lo scoiattolo ha una pancia morbida.

Chipmunk har en myk mage.

The chipmunk has a soft tummy.

La tamia ha portato a casa una ghianda gigante.

Chipmunk brakte hjem en gigantisk eikenøtt.

The chipmunk brought home a giant acorn.

I Can...

- [ ] read the 1st sentence.
- [ ] read the 2nd sentence.
- [ ] read the 3rd sentence.
- [ ] make my own sentence.
- [ ] color a picture.

Ho dieci dita in totale.

Jeg har ti tær totalt.

I have ten toes in total.

Uno e Zero insieme sono dieci.

One og Zero sammen er ti.

One and Zero together are ten.

Name

I Can...

- [ ] read the 1st sentence.
- [ ] read the 2nd sentence.
- [ ] read the 3rd sentence.
- [ ] make my own sentence.
- [ ] color a picture.

L'alligatore sta saltando.

Alligatoren hopper.

The alligator is jumping.

Il coccodrillo che salta è felice.

Den hoppende krokodillen er fornøyd.

The jumping crocodile is happy.

Name

I Can...

- ☐ read the 1st sentence.
- ☐ read the 2nd sentence.
- ☐ read the 3rd sentence.
- ☐ make my own sentence.
- ☐ color a picture.

Ho trovato una formica.

Jeg fant en maur.

I found an ant.

Una formica è di taglia piccola, ma molto forte.

En maur er liten i størrelse, men veldig sterk.

An ant is tiny in size, but very strong.

Name 

I Can...

- [ ] read the 1st sentence.
- [ ] read the 2nd sentence.
- [ ] read the 3rd sentence.
- [ ] make my own sentence.
- [ ] color a picture.

Il pipistrello dorme a testa in giù.

Flaggermusen sover opp ned.

The bat sleeps upside down.

Il pipistrello abbraccia la lettera.

Flaggermusen klemmer brevet.

The bat is hugging the letter.

Name ________________________

I Can...

- [ ] read the 1st sentence.
- [ ] read the 2nd sentence.
- [ ] read the 3rd sentence.
- [ ] make my own sentence.
- [ ] color a picture.

Il gatto è molto stanco.

Katten er veldig sliten.

The cat is very tired.

Il gatto ha molto sonno.

Katten er veldig søvnig.

The cat is very sleepy.

Name

I Can...

- [ ] read the 1st sentence.
- [ ] read the 2nd sentence.
- [ ] read the 3rd sentence.
- [ ] make my own sentence.
- [ ] color a picture.

Al cane piace giocare.

Hunden liker å leke.

The dog likes to play.

Al cane piace leccare l'osso.

Hunden liker å slikke beinet.

The dog likes to lick the bone.

Name _______________ 

I Can...

- [ ] read the 1st sentence.
- [ ] read the 2nd sentence.
- [ ] read the 3rd sentence.
- [ ] make my own sentence.
- [ ] color a picture.

L'elefante ha le ciglia.

Elefanten har øyevipper.

The elephant has eyelashes.

L'elefante ha orecchie grandi.

Elefanten har store ører.

The elephant has big ears.

Name

I Can...

- [ ] read the 1st sentence.
- [ ] read the 2nd sentence.
- [ ] read the 3rd sentence.
- [ ] make my own sentence.
- [ ] color a picture.

La rana sta saltellando.

Frosken hopper.

The frog is hopping.

La rana usa la lingua per catturare la preda.

Frosken bruker tungen for å fange byttedyr.

The frog uses its tongue to catch prey.

Name

I Can...

- [ ] read the 1st sentence.
- [ ] read the 2nd sentence.
- [ ] read the 3rd sentence.
- [ ] make my own sentence.
- [ ] color a picture.

La capra cammina assonnata.

Geita går søvnig rundt.

The goat is sleepily walking around.

La capra sta pascendo nel prato.

Geita beiter på engen.

The goat is grazing in the meadow.

Name ______________________ 

I Can...

- [ ] read the 1st sentence.
- [ ] read the 2nd sentence.
- [ ] read the 3rd sentence.
- [ ] make my own sentence.
- [ ] color a picture.

L'ippopotamo ha una testa grande.

Flodhesten har et stort hode.

The hippo has a big head.

L'ippopotamo è stupito di quanto siano grandi i suoi denti.

Flodhesten er overrasket over hvor store tennene hans er.

The hippo is amazed at how big his teeth are.

Name

I Can...

- [ ] read the 1st sentence.
- [ ] read the 2nd sentence.
- [ ] read the 3rd sentence.
- [ ] make my own sentence.
- [ ] color a picture.

L'iguana ha una coda lunga.

Leguanen har en lang hale.

The iguana has a long tail.

L'iguana si sta avvolgendo attorno all'alfabeto.

Leguanen krøller seg rundt alfabetet.

The iguana is curling around the alphabet.

Name ___________________________ 

I Can...

- [ ] read the 1st sentence.
- [ ] read the 2nd sentence.
- [ ] read the 3rd sentence.
- [ ] make my own sentence.
- [ ] color a picture.

La mamma ha comprato una nuova bottiglia di marmellata.

Mamma kjøpte en ny flaske syltetøy.

Mom bought a new bottle of jam.

Puoi mettere la marmellata sul toast per dargli più gusto.

Du kan legge syltetøy på toast for å gi den mer smak.

You can put jam on toast to give it more taste.

Name

I Can...

- [ ] read the 1st sentence.
- [ ] read the 2nd sentence.
- [ ] read the 3rd sentence.
- [ ] make my own sentence.
- [ ] color a picture.

L'aquilone ha una bellissima coda.

Kiten har en vakker hale.

The kite has a beautiful tail.

L'aquilone è a terra.

Kiten er på bakken.

The kite is on the ground.

Name

I Can...

- [ ] read the 1st sentence.
- [ ] read the 2nd sentence.
- [ ] read the 3rd sentence.
- [ ] make my own sentence.
- [ ] color a picture.

Il leone è timido.

Løven er redd.

The lion is timid.

Il leone sta inseguendo la coda.

Løven jager halen.

The lion is chasing its tail.

Name

I Can...

- [ ] read the 1st sentence.
- [ ] read the 2nd sentence.
- [ ] read the 3rd sentence.
- [ ] make my own sentence.
- [ ] color a picture.

Mi piacciono i topi.

Jeg liker mus.

I like mice.

Il mouse ha baffi molto lunghi.

Musen har veldig lange værhår.

The mouse has very long whiskers.

Name

I Can...

- [ ] read the 1st sentence.
- [ ] read the 2nd sentence.
- [ ] read the 3rd sentence.
- [ ] make my own sentence.
- [ ] color a picture.

Il naso sta respirando.

Nesen puster.

The nose is breathing.

Il naso è usato per annusare le cose.

Nesen brukes til å lukte ting.

The nose is used for smelling things.

Name ___________________________ 

I Can...

- [ ] read the 1st sentence.
- [ ] read the 2nd sentence.
- [ ] read the 3rd sentence.
- [ ] make my own sentence.
- [ ] color a picture.

Il polpo vive sott'acqua.

Blekkspruten lever under vann.

The octopus lives underwater.

Il polpo ha tentacoli molto lunghi.

Blekkspruten har veldig lange tentakler.

The octopus has very long tentacles.

Name ________________________

I Can...

- [ ] read the 1st sentence.
- [ ] read the 2nd sentence.
- [ ] read the 3rd sentence.
- [ ] make my own sentence.
- [ ] color a picture.

Il pinguino mangia pesce.

Pingvinen spiser fisk.

The penguin eats fish.

Il pinguino vive nelle regioni fredde.

Pingvinen bor i kalde strøk.

The penguin lives in cold regions.

Name

I Can...

- [ ] read the 1st sentence.
- [ ] read the 2nd sentence.
- [ ] read the 3rd sentence.
- [ ] make my own sentence.
- [ ] color a picture.

La regina ha una bacchetta.

Dronningen har en tryllestav.

The queen has a wand.

La regina ha una bacchetta rosa.

Dronningen har en rosa stav.

The queen has a pink wand.

Name ______________________

I Can...

- ☐ read the 1st sentence.
- ☐ read the 2nd sentence.
- ☐ read the 3rd sentence.
- ☐ make my own sentence.
- ☐ color a picture.

Il coniglio ha le orecchie lunghe.

Kaninen har lange ører.

The rabbit has long ears.

Il coniglio è confuso.

Kaninen er forvirret.

The rabbit is confused.

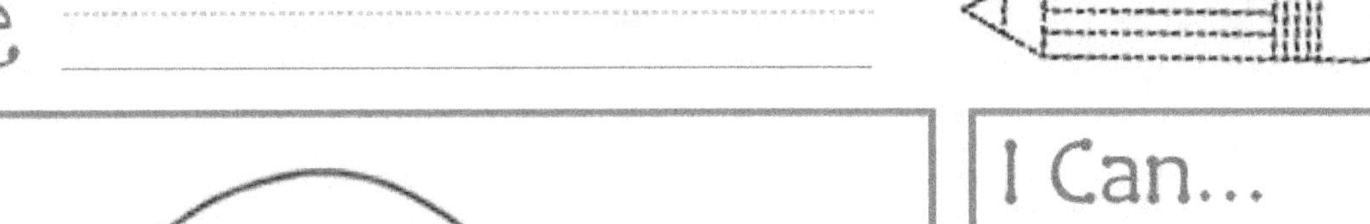

I Can...

- [ ] read the 1st sentence.
- [ ] read the 2nd sentence.
- [ ] read the 3rd sentence.
- [ ] make my own sentence.
- [ ] color a picture.

Il serpente ha pois.

Slangen har prikker.

The snake has polka dots.

Il serpente è molto viscido.

Slangen er veldig slim.

The snake is very slimy.

Name ______________________

I Can...

- [ ] read the 1st sentence.
- [ ] read the 2nd sentence.
- [ ] read the 3rd sentence.
- [ ] make my own sentence.
- [ ] color a picture.

La tartaruga ha un guscio appuntito.

Skilpadden har et spisse skall.

The tortoise has a pointy shell.

La tartaruga vive sulla terra, a differenza delle tartarughe.

Skilpadden lever på land, i motsetning til skilpadder.

The tortoise lives on land, unlike turtles.

Name

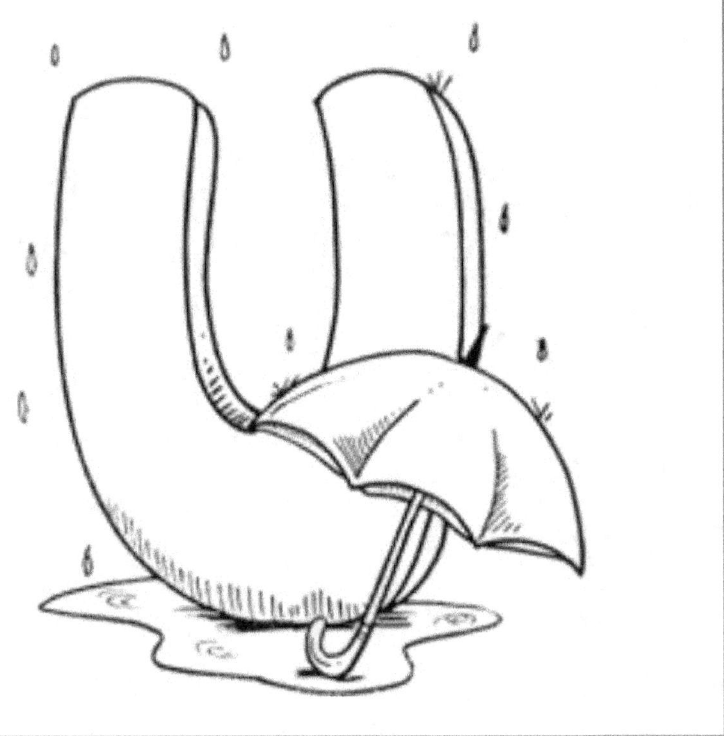

I Can...

- [ ] read the 1st sentence.
- [ ] read the 2nd sentence.
- [ ] read the 3rd sentence.
- [ ] make my own sentence.
- [ ] color a picture.

Piove.

Det regner.

It's raining.

L'ombrello ti protegge.

Paraplyen skjuler deg.

The umbrella shelters you.

Name

I Can...

- ☐ read the 1st sentence.
- ☐ read the 2nd sentence.
- ☐ read the 3rd sentence.
- ☐ make my own sentence.
- ☐ color a picture.

Il violino è uno strumento musicale.

Fiolinen er et musikkinstrument.

The violin is a musical instrument.

Il violino è uno degli strumenti più fantastici.

Fiolin er et av de mest fantastiske instrumentene.

The violin is one of the most fantastic instruments.

Name ___________

I Can...

- [ ] read the 1st sentence.
- [ ] read the 2nd sentence.
- [ ] read the 3rd sentence.
- [ ] make my own sentence.
- [ ] color a picture.

Il tricheco ha un amico.

Hvalrossen har en venn.

The walrus has a friend.

Il tricheco ha una coda.

Hvalrossen har en hale.

The walrus has a tail.

Name ___________________________

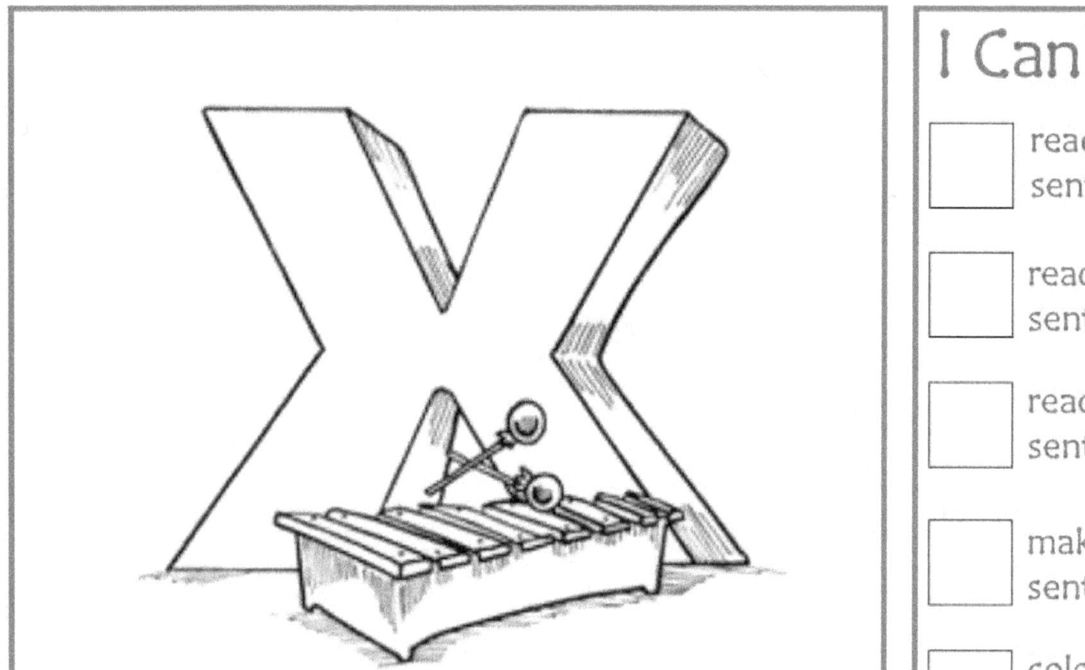

I Can...

- [ ] read the 1st sentence.
- [ ] read the 2nd sentence.
- [ ] read the 3rd sentence.
- [ ] make my own sentence.
- [ ] color a picture.

Lo xilofono è uno strumento colorato.

Xylofonen er et fargerikt instrument.

The xylophone is a colorful instrument.

Lo xilofono è uno strumento molto interessante.

Xylofonen er et veldig kult instrument.

The xylophone is a very cool instrument.

Name _______________ 

I Can...

- [ ] read the 1st sentence.
- [ ] read the 2nd sentence.
- [ ] read the 3rd sentence.
- [ ] make my own sentence.
- [ ] color a picture.

Il ragazzo ha un cappellino.

Gutten har en liten hatt.

The boy has a little hat.

Il bambino ha uno yoyo molto colorato.

Barnet har en veldig fargerik yoyo.

The kid has a very colorful yoyo.

Name _______________________

I Can...

- ☐ read the 1st sentence.
- ☐ read the 2nd sentence.
- ☐ read the 3rd sentence.
- ☐ make my own sentence.
- ☐ color a picture.

La zebra ha una coda.

Sebraen har en hale.

The zebra has a tail.

La zebra sorride ampiamente

Sebraen smiler bredt

The zebra is smiling widely

Name _______________________

I Can...

- [ ] read the 1st sentence.
- [ ] read the 2nd sentence.
- [ ] read the 3rd sentence.
- [ ] make my own sentence.
- [ ] color a picture.

Ho una candela sulla mia torta.

Jeg har et lys på kaken.

I have a candle on my cake.

Questa torta di compleanno è per un bambino.

Denne bursdagskaken er for et lite barn.

This birthday cake is for a little kids.

Name ___________________________ 

I Can...

- [ ] read the 1st sentence.
- [ ] read the 2nd sentence.
- [ ] read the 3rd sentence.
- [ ] make my own sentence.
- [ ] color a picture.

L'astronauta sta andando in missione.

Astronauten skal på oppdrag.

The astronaut is going on a mission.

L'astronauta vide qualcosa in lontananza.

Astronauten så noe i det fjerne.

The astronaut saw something in the distance.

Name

I Can...

- [ ] read the 1st sentence.
- [ ] read the 2nd sentence.
- [ ] read the 3rd sentence.
- [ ] make my own sentence.
- [ ] color a picture.

Il samurai sta andando a fare jogging mattutino.

Samurai skal på morgenjoggetur.

The samurai is going for a morning jog.

Il samurai sta inseguendo il suo nemico.

Samuraien jager bort fienden.

The samurai is chasing away his enemy.

I Can...

- [ ] read the 1st sentence.
- [ ] read the 2nd sentence.
- [ ] read the 3rd sentence.
- [ ] make my own sentence.
- [ ] color a picture.

Il mio amico sta mangiando una torta gigantesca.

Venninnen min har en gigantisk kake.

My friend is having a gigantic cake.

Questa torta di compleanno ha tre strati.

Denne bursdagskaken har tre lag.

This birthday cake has three layers.

Name _______________

I Can...

- [ ] read the 1st sentence.
- [ ] read the 2nd sentence.
- [ ] read the 3rd sentence.
- [ ] make my own sentence.
- [ ] color a picture.

La rana sta inseguendo la mosca.

Frosken jager flua.

The frog is chasing the fly.

La rana sta prendendo una mosca.

Frosken fanger en flue.

The frog is catching a fly.

www.ingramcontent.com/pod-product-compliance
Lightning Source LLC
Chambersburg PA
CBHW080836160726
47999CB00009B/2916